Kelen Campos Benito

Moral Damage in Social Security Benefits

Kelen Campos Benito

Moral Damage in Social Security Benefits

And Its Resulting Vices

ScienciaScripts

Imprint

Any brand names and product names mentioned in this book are subject to trademark, brand or patent protection and are trademarks or registered trademarks of their respective holders. The use of brand names, product names, common names, trade names, product descriptions etc. even without a particular marking in this work is in no way to be construed to mean that such names may be regarded as unrestricted in respect of trademark and brand protection legislation and could thus be used by anyone.

Cover image: www.ingimage.com

This book is a translation from the original published under ISBN 978-613-9-72553-3.

Publisher:
Sciencia Scripts
is a trademark of
Dodo Books Indian Ocean Ltd. and OmniScriptum S.R.L publishing group

120 High Road, East Finchley, London, N2 9ED, United Kingdom
Str. Armeneasca 28/1, office 1, Chisinau MD-2012, Republic of Moldova, Europe
Printed at: see last page
ISBN: 978-620-7-74026-0

Copyright © Kelen Campos Benito
Copyright © 2024 Dodo Books Indian Ocean Ltd. and OmniScriptum S.R.L publishing group

SUMMARY

This bibliographical research paper deals with moral damages in social security benefits by analysing possible damages resulting from defects and irregularities detected in the granting of social security benefits. Firstly, it studies moral damage in social security law and the characterisation of social security rights as fundamental social rights and the alimentary nature of social security benefits, as well as those responsible for defects resulting from moral damage in social security law and its principles. Secondly, the social security benefits and the types of defects that give rise to moral damage are studied. We also study the identification of moral damage resulting from defects in the granting of social security benefits, the configuration of social security moral damage and its reparation.

Key words: Social security law. Social Security Benefits. Moral Damage.

SUMMARY

INTRODUCTION

This work aims to address the issue of moral damage in social security law, with the objective of analysing the institute of moral damage in social security benefits and its reparation.

The general aim of this work is to demonstrate how moral damage occurs in social security benefits, as well as the state's responsibility towards the insured. As a specific objective, the work aims to study what moral damage is and how it occurs in social security law and in social security benefits. It also aims to verify the State's responsibility in the face of moral damage in social security benefits, as well as the role of constitutional and social security principles. It also aims to analyse what social security benefits are and the occurrence of moral damage in these benefits.

The proposed theme will be divided into two chapters, in which the following subjects will be studied: Moral damage in social security law; who is responsible for the damage in social security law, the principles of social security, the application of moral damage in social security benefits, social security benefits and the defects that give rise to moral damage in social security benefits.

The first chapter will study what moral damage is and how it occurs in social security law. It will also analyse the state's responsibility in relation to moral damage in social security benefits, as well as the principles that govern social security.

In the second chapter, the social security benefits and the reasons that give rise to moral damage in social security benefits will be studied. The administrative procedure for granting social security benefits is examined. The case law on defects in social security benefits is also discussed.

Therefore, this study aims to point out the failings of the administration in the granting of social security benefits, which generates the need for compensation for moral damage resulting from the state's civil liability, as well as presenting ways of correcting, through the imposition of the duty to repair, practices that are harmful to insured people and those dependent on social security.

1. MORAL DAMAGE IN SOCIAL SECURITY LAW

According to Martinez (2005, p.30) "there is no legal concept in the legal sphere in general, and even less so in relation to social security. Thus, there is no definition of social security moral damage. It can be said that it occurs within the orbit of social protection and nothing more".

This thesis is corroborated by Farineli, et.al (2011, p. 99) "The scarcity of scientific production on this important subject is notorious, and the case law of our courts is still controversial."

The victim will be the same as for other injuries, but the perpetrator will be different. We must not forget the need of those seeking social protection, as if it were a dream, supported by the subjective right, and if injury occurs it must be repaired in proportion to the damage.

The right to social security is a social and fundamental right, which is why means must be found to protect it, which, if violated, can be done through moral damage. Following the generational classification of fundamental rights, the right to social security would fall into the second generation. With regard to social security rights:

> Social security rights are fundamental rights that aim to safeguard the principle chosen as the foundation of the Republic: the Dignity of the Human Person, relating to the insured person who, affected by a misfortune, is unable to support themselves and their family through their labour power. In this condition, the insured person of the General Social Security Scheme, affected by one of the contingencies provided for by law, or their dependant, must be covered by social security, with a view to guaranteeing their right to survival with dignity (HENK, 2012, p. 291).

The social security right, as a social and fundamental right, is being included in the process of declaration and realisation, having its immediate applicability, and means must be found for its protection, this being through indemnity for moral damage. According to Campos:

> One of the ways of making social security rights effective, by taking integrated action in the judicial sphere, is to guarantee their protection

against defects in the process and the administrative act of granting benefits, which were analysed in the previous chapter, by imposing moral reparation to be borne by the INSS when it causes moral distress to insured people and their dependents (CAMPOS, 2011, p.82).

The authors Farineli and Maschieto also agree:

The right to social security is a fundamental human right. Following the generational classification of fundamental rights, the right to social security would fall under the second generation. The main landmarks of second generation fundamental rights were the Mexican Constitution of 1917 and the German Constitution of 1919. Second generation rights include economic and social rights (FARINELI, et.al, 2011, p. 36).

The definition of moral damage in social security law has not yet been perfectly defined, but the idea of social security benefits being alimentary is widely accepted by the doctrine. In this sense:

Social security rights are basic rights for people's survival, they have a food nature, they must be applied immediately when the triggering event occurs and their realisation must be concrete, respecting the Principle of the Dignity of the Human Person (FARINELI, et.al, 2011, p.92).

Thus, the social security benefit has the idea of food in the same way that the welfare benefit preserves means of subsistence. According to Campos:

Social security benefits are of a food nature, since they are used to cover the basic vital needs of human beings and their families, such as housing, food, health, transport, hygiene, clothing and education, among others (CAMPOS, 2011, p. 76,77).

The food nature of social security benefits is fundamental in social law, as it is part of the fundamental rights of human beings, as it creates conditions of survival for people who are experiencing difficulties in their lives. Henk corroborates this thesis:

> The right to social security benefits is a fundamental social right, of a food nature, whose function is to guarantee the dignified subsistence of the insured person who faces some contingency and thus finds themselves unable to support themselves by their own labour power. It is a fundamental right closely linked to maintaining the dignity of the human person, which it must protect and guarantee (HENK, 2012, p. 290).

The concept of moral damage in social security law is the same as in civil law, where the damage affects the person, their property, in the individual sphere, affecting their personality:

> It seems more reasonable, therefore, to characterise moral damage by its own elements; therefore, "as the deprivation or diminution of those goods that have a primary value in the life of man and which are peace, tranquillity of mind, individual freedom, individual integrity, physical integrity, honour and other sacred affections" (CAHALI, 1999, p.20).

According to Esteves, et.al (1999, p. 33) Internal moral damage causes serious, possibly irreversible and even lethal psychological injuries. In these circumstances, internal moral damage must be respected, and in certain situations the extent and consequences must be ascertained through evidence.

The subjective element must be verified, i.e. the offender's intent or guilt, the repercussions of the offence, the suffering caused to the offended party, in order for moral compensation to be set.

Brazilian legislation does not yet offer a concept of moral damage. Ordinary legislation has not yet endeavoured to define it, configure it or describe what it means to be moral damage, but the doctrine has done so. The Civil Code itself is generic in this respect and is not a useful indication. Corroborating this thesis:

> It is for no other reason that the reparability of moral damage, already definitively accepted by national and foreign doctrine as a thesis, had been affirmed and reaffirmed by the jurisprudence of our courts, as having been accepted by our private law (CAHALI, 1999, p.55)

According to Cahali (1999, p. 29) "The principle of the reparability of moral damages has been gradually enshrined in most civilised countries, with their legislation varying only in terms of the extent to which they grant it".

The Consolidation of Labour Laws (CLT), although there are several cases of moral damage, does not include this concept in labour law. In social security law, as mentioned above, the concept is non-existent. The Civil Code itself contained a limited concept of moral damage. According to Cahali:

> From this text, it could be inferred that the author of the draft code recognised the reparability of moral damage, but limited it to those cases provided for in the chapter on the settlement of obligations resulting from unlawful acts (CAHALI, 1999, p. 45).

Therefore, the idea of reparation for moral damage is lacking, which would allow the obligation to indemnify in each case to be syllogised, but even so the agent would not be exempt from repairing the damage caused.

There was a definition of property damage in the main codes of civilisations, but over time it was discovered that moral damage should also be repaired, because according to Martinez (2005, p.22) "man contained within himself an incorporeal value, perhaps greater, represented by his freedom, honour, dignity, etc".

The solution found to try to reduce moral injury was to punish the perpetrator with a pecuniary penalty in favour of the offended party, or by providing community services. According to Bittar:

> If there is damage, unjustly produced in the sphere of others, the need for reparation arises, as a natural imposition of life in society and, precisely, for its own existence and the normal development of the potential of each personalised entity (BITTAR, 1997, p. 20).

Moral damage is often defined by exclusion as something that is not property, but this concept is considered incomplete, as the remaining spectrum is very broad.

In the case of pecuniary damage, the equivalent value of the damage in money is sought, fully compensating the offended party, restoring the offended party's assets to their previous state as if the injury had not occurred.

In moral damage, the damage is not resolved in compensation, because compensation is the elimination of damage, which is not possible when it comes to moral damage. According to Cahali:

> Under these conditions, therefore, the ontological basis of compensation for moral damages does not differ substantially, if at all in degree, from the legal basis of compensation for pecuniary damage, remaining intrinsic in both the sanctioning and afflictive characters stylised by modern law (CAHALI, 1999, p. 39).

Doctrine and jurisprudence are unanimous in stating that it is possible to cumulate moral damage and material damage for the same fact, since it is possible to state that the same fact can cause damage in both the moral and material spheres.

Moral damage is related to the individual's intimate sphere and is therefore difficult to ascertain. It is an injury that affects morale and disturbs the victim's peace of mind. With regard to damage:

> It is important to emphasise that moral damage is not ordinary annoyance or mere dissatisfaction. In order for moral damage to be characterised, it is necessary to be faced with a situation that goes beyond what is socially acceptable. It is necessary that the agent's conduct causes intense negative emotion to the injured party, shaking their normal psyche (FARINELI, et.al, 2011, p.112, 113).

Moral damage occurs because of the sphere of subjectivity, or the value of the person in society, in which a fact has repercussions, affecting the most intimate aspects of the human personality. In this sense, Bittar says

> On this level, it is clear that harmful actions or omissions disrupt the balance that exists in the factual world, physically, morally or pecuniarily burdening the injured parties, who, in the face of the respective injustice, are ipso facto invested with powers to defend the interests that have been violated, at different levels and in the light of the circumstances of the specific case. Law is responsible for preserving people's moral and patrimonial integrity, maintaining balance in the social environment and in the individual sphere of each member of the community, in their incessant search for personal happiness". (BITTAR, 1997, p.15.)

According to Campos (2010, p.83), moral damage is not perfectly recoverable, because moral suffering cannot be recovered, it is irreversible and reparation is clearly a sanction for the offender and a way of minimising the consequences.

For Cavalieri (2009, p.81) moral damage is no longer restricted to pain, sadness and suffering, but extends to all personal property, which is why it is more appropriate to call it immaterial or non-pecuniary damage.

Moral damage is not susceptible to pecuniary evaluation and can only be compensated by the pecuniary obligation imposed on the person who caused the damage, which is more like satisfaction than compensation. According to Cahali:

> To say that it is repugnant to morality to repair the pain of others with money is to displace the issue, because it is not intended to sell a moral good, but simply to maintain that this good, like all others, must be respected; when the victim claims pecuniary reparation for moral damage, he is not asking for a price for his pain, but only for a means of partially mitigating the consequences of the legal injury (CAHALI, 1999, p. 26).

According to Martinez (2005, p.29) "The difficulty lies in the fact that everyone has their own concept of what morals, honour and principles are, and each person's conception differs from the social average". The Civil Code itself failed to include a general rule for compensation for moral damage.

Any unjust damage suffered by a person must find a response in the legal system. There are damages to personality rights that are only reflected in the patrimonial orbit, or are mixed with others in the moral orbit. According to Bittar:

> Moral damages are those that affect the most intimate aspects of the human personality (intimacy and personal consideration), or the person's own valuation in the environment in which they live and act (reputation or social consideration) (BITTAR, 1997, p. 45).

Personality is the main attribute of the human being, and in view of the different provisions that protect it, reparation when there is an offence is a right of the person, and is, moreover, a constitutional guarantee. According to Martinez:

> Moral damage is an unlawful act committed by a human being, on their

> behalf or on behalf of a legal person, knowingly or unknowingly, omissively or commissively, which objectively affects the personality of the subject of that action, causing them personal or social embarrassment, a naturally measurable offence, a reduction in their assets as a citizen, which can be timely and legally repaired (MARTINEZ, 2005, p.29).

For Esteves, et.al (1999, p.33), the concept of moral damage is in line with the Civil Code, stating that moral damage, in its internal and external aspects, must be well described in the initial petition, to make it possible to assess the offender's intent or guilt, its repercussions, the suffering of the injured party, in order to set the compensation.

The theme of moral damage is located in the theory of civil liability, considering the person themselves or their social projection, individualising the damage in the injuries caused. According to Bittar:

> In fact, the human personality unfolds through different attributes, of a physical, psychic or moral nature. But, briefly, the person can be considered in their psyche or in the sphere of social consideration, presenting themselves, in the first hypothesis, as a reactor to external stimuli, with their intelligence (sphere of knowledge and representation), with their active elements (pleasant or unpleasant states that representations provoke); and in the second hypothesis, as an object of analysis, or of appreciation by others, or even as a being susceptible to social valuation (by the collectivity, by a group or even by any person) (BITTAR, 1997, p.47).

As a result, moral damages are on a factual level, as injuries to the human personality, situated within the scope of the human being, moral damages both to individuals and to legal entities, reaching the psyche and personality of the injured being.

Thus, the consequences of harmful acts affect certain facets of the injured party's legal sphere. From a moral point of view, the injury can result in moral aggression or an attack on the injured party's assets.

Therefore, the action to repair the damage must be aimed at exhausting its potential, the unpleasant sensations suffered, according to the specific case. With regard to repairing the damage:

> The right to reparation is attached to damages of the most diverse nature,

> which can arise from different external and internal stimuli, due to the complexity of social life, the extent of possible relationships and the infinite potential of human intelligence (BITTAR, 1997, p.29).

Moral reparation goes beyond pecuniary reparation, without considering the difficulties of assessing the damage and quantifying it. Most of the time, it is impossible to restore the damage suffered to its previous state, and it is up to the legislator to estimate it on a case-by-case basis.

In this respect, only pain, vexation, suffering and humiliation that goes beyond normality, that interferes with the subject's psychological behaviour, that causes them such distress and imbalance in their well-being, should be considered moral damage. In this context:

> The harm caused by the crime may simply consist of physical or moral suffering, with no direct relation to the offended party's assets, such as that resulting from a minor injury that does not prevent one from exercising one's profession, or from an attack on honour (CAHALI, 1999, p. 43)

Moral damage is an injury to the sphere of human personality situated in the sphere of the human being as a thinking being who reacts to social interactions; in fact, the human personality is broken down into different attributes of a physical, psychological or moral nature.

The state will always be objectively liable for damage caused to third parties by the action or omission of its agents. Once the victim has been compensated, the state will bring a regressive action against the person who caused the damage.

1.1. Responsible for Damages in Social Security Law

According to Farineli, et.al (2011 p. 49) "in the early days of human civilisation, civil liability was based on collective revenge, which was characterised by the group's joint reaction against the aggressor".

Over time, the institute evolved into a private vendetta in which justice was taken into one's own hands. The government intervened only to dictate how and when the victim could retaliate against the offender in the same proportion as the offence.

With the passage of time came the idea of composing the conflict by making reparation through punishment and other assets. After this phase came the idea of legal composition, in which the offender was punished by the state.

The theory of strict liability was materialised through doctrine, with those responsible for the principle of civil liability influencing almost all legislation. In this context:

> The breadth of the concept of civil liability reveals difficulties in sticking to a single definition, because the doctrine tends to unite technical concepts and the concrete reality of the obligation to repair damage, regardless of whether they are identified with causality, subjective or objective theory (FARINELI, et.al, 2011, p. 53).

The field of civil liability is broad, as it is not just a legal institute of civil law; it is normal for it to undergo the natural adaptations of public and private law, while maintaining its legal unity.

The purpose of civil liability is to restore the balance violated by the damage. For this reason, civil liability exists in our legal system not only as an idea of wrongdoing, but also as compensation for damages.

Contemporary civil liability is one that seeks to repair the injured party to their previous state, with a dual function of maintaining legal certainty and applying a civil penalty of a compensatory nature.

In social security law, it is common for the person responsible for the damage to be a legal person, with the undesired illicit result being enough, regardless of the presence of intent or guilt, playing an educational role and not just compensating the victim:

> The purpose of moral damages is not just to compensate the victim for their psychological losses. It has an educational role, which is superior, because it is social, to discourage offences. Bearing in mind that the State's ability to compensate is presumed, the judge can set the quantum in two parts: a) compensatory for the victim and b) educational for the perpetrator (MARTINEZ, 2005, p. 65).

According to Di Pietro (2008, p.57), the objective responsibility of the state is linked to administrative risk. For there to be liability, it is necessary to demonstrate the conduct of the public entity, whether negative or positive, whether omission or action, the damage and the causal link between these elements. In addition, it is important that there is no exclusion, represented by the fact/blame of the victim or a third party, unforeseeable circumstances or force majeure.

Mere dissatisfaction is therefore outside the orbit of moral damage, as it is part of the normality of everyday life, and is not an intense and lasting situation to the point of shaking the individual's psyche. If this is not understood in this way, it could trivialise the institute of moral damage. In this sense:

> The right to reparation is intended for the most diverse types of damage that can arise from different external and internal stimuli, due to the complexity of social life, the extent of possible relationships and the infinite potential of human intelligence (BITTAR, 1997, p. 29).

Civil liability for the commissive act of the National Social Security Institute is objective, as it is a service-providing Autarchy, and also depends on conduct, damage and causal link. The National Social Security Institute (INSS) is essential not only for its insured members, but for society as a whole.

Moral damage is related to the individual's privacy, and is therefore difficult to ascertain, with repercussions on the individual's morale and mental tranquillity. This thesis is corroborated:

> Moral damage is an unlawful act committed by a human being, on their behalf or on behalf of a legal person, knowingly or unknowingly, omissively or commissively, which objectively affects the personality of the subject of that action, causing them personal or social embarrassment, a naturally measurable offence, a reduction in their assets as a citizen, which can be timely and legally repaired (MARTINEZ, 2005, p.29).

The difficulty is in identifying the damage, and this is not enough for it to go unrepaired, since if there is damage to the person, the refusal to protect life, health, physical integrity, morals, freedom, honour, is subject to civil reparation. In Cahali's view:

> When it comes to objecting to the impossibility of compensating damage of this nature on a civil level, i.e. using the criterion of equivalence, it should be borne in mind that equivalence is not required here in absolute terms, insofar as compensation is merely satisfactory (CAHALI, 1999, p. 26).

Damage is the prerequisite for civil liability, which is understood as the injury experienced by the victim to their complex of legal, material or moral assets. Corroborating this thesis:

> Liability therefore depends on proving that the harmful result (damage) is the result of the action of the injured party (unlawful action or omission) and its effect or consequence (causal or etiological link). It is therefore necessary to verify the prior existence of damage to the injured party's legal sphere, in order to recompense or compensate them, they can use the instruments of reaction that are appropriate when applying the theory in question, even when the damage is of a moral nature (BITTAR, 1997, p. 17).

Thus, damage is an unjust injury to components of values protected by the law, including moral damage. If there is damage, unjustly produced in the sphere of others, the need for reparation arises.

The reparability of moral damage, if awarded compensation, would be a penalty, incompatible with private law, since it does not vary the recomposition of the offended party's assets. According to Cahali:

> In the reparation of moral damages, money does not fulfil the function of equivalence, as in the case of material damages, but, concomitantly, the satisfactory function is the penalty. Thus, the offended party's civil liability results in the right to compensation for the damage (in the generic sense), which is resolved either by compensation for property damage or by compensation for moral damage (CAHALI, 1999, p. 41,42).

According to Theodoro Agostinho, "Jurisprudence, as an informing source of law, has been decisive in the viability of intangible civil reparation within the social security concept discussed here, supporting the evolution of civil reparation within this branch of legal science."

The best way to verify the occurrence of moral damage is to weigh up the effects of the situation on an average man, who would be far from cold and extremely sensitive.

The state is obliged to compensate insured persons for moral damage in the event of defects in the granting of social security benefits or defects in the collection of social security taxes that cause damage to insured persons or taxpayers. Along these lines:

> Well-being, which translates into the promotion of the human person, is the system's driving force, capable of justifying its existence and driving its synchronised movements. Without this driving force, the system would be reduced to a simple aggregate of the state organism (BALERA, 2006, p.18)

According to Zimmermann (2011, p. 11) "The State is liable for damages caused to others as a result of actions or omissions carried out by its agents as a result of public administration activities". The State's responsibility has the power to curb abusive practices caused to policyholders.

The case law of the Superior Court of Justice (STJ) deals with state responsibility:

> STATE LIABILITY. INDEMNITY FOR MORAL DAMAGES. DEATH OF INSURED WOMAN. SUSPENSION OF SICKNESS BENEFIT. CAUSAL LINK ESTABLISHED IN THE ORDINARY INSTANCE. REVIEW. IMPOSSIBILITY. SUMMULA 7/STJ. REDUCTION OF THE QUANTUM. POSSIBILITY IN THIS CASE. EXORBITANT AMOUNT. PRECEDENTS.
>
> I - This is a lawsuit filed against the INSS, seeking compensation for moral damages resulting from the death of the plaintiffs' wife and mother, related to the cancellation of the sickness benefit by the social security agency, and the request was accepted by the Regional Court a quo.
>
> II - This Court of Justice, however, allows for a review of the amount set in this regard when it is derisory or exorbitant. Therefore, the amount set by the lower court (approximately 900 minimum wages at the time) should be reduced to bring it into line with this Court's case law, setting the compensation at 300 minimum wages. Precedents: REsp n° 737.797/RJ, Rel. Min. LUIZ FUX, DJ of 28.08.06, REsp n° 790.090/RR, Rel. Min. DENISE ARRUDA, DJ of 10.09.07, among others.

III - Appeal partially recognised and upheld.[1]

This objective is the raison d'être of the state, which requires the implementation of projects in relation to social security and assistance plans for the insured and dependents of Social Security. With regard to state responsibility:

> For this reason, it is necessary to analyse the responsibility of the state, especially the National Social Security Institute (INSS), in conducting and granting social security benefits and the defects arising from the process and the administrative act of granting social security benefits, as well as the responsibility of the federal government in collecting, supervising and charging contributions (CAMPOS, 2011, p.79).

The state must ensure that social security benefits are granted without defects and that contributions are made correctly, because all of this represents legal certainty for social security insured people and their dependents.

The state's responsibility can be either contractual, which derives from the will of the parties, or non-contractual, which has an institutional character and does not depend on the will of the parties, but of the community. In this sense:

> The state will always be objectively liable for the damage caused to the public servant by the action or omission of its agents, as long as it does not recognise one of the exclusions of state liability. Once the victim has been compensated, the state will bring a regressive action against the agent who caused the damage, if the latter is guilty or wilful (FARINELI, et.al, 2011, p.94, 95).

Thus, the state's responsibility is non-contractual, it does not depend on the will of the parties, it is imposed by the institution and accepted by the community, deriving from a relationship between the insured and the INSS. Corroborating this thesis:

> [...] the obligation to repair the damage is independent of proving the fault

---

[1] REsp 1026088 / SC, RECURSO ESPECIAL, 2008/0023141-0, Rapporteur, Minister FRANCISCO FALCÃO (1116)Órgão Julgador, T1 - PRIMEIRA TURMA, Date of Judgement, 03/04/2008, Date of Publication/Source, DJe, 23/04/2008

> or intent of the public agent in the active or omissive conduct. The state must repair or indemnify the damage, without knowing the reason for the agent's harmful behaviour, whether or not they made a mistake, whether or not they acted with due care, other than to sue them on a regressive basis, but these circumstances cannot be invoked against the victims (CAMPOS, 2011, p. 89).

The civil liability of the state can be objective or subjective. Objective liability is independent of fault, i.e. it is linked to the actions of the state and its agents, while subjective liability depends on fault, i.e. it derives from the omission of its agents.

The state will always be objectively liable for the damage caused to the insured by the action or omission of its agents, and once the victimised insured has been compensated, the state will bring a regressive action against the insured.

In subjective civil liability it is necessary to prove the agent's intent or fault. With regard to civil liability:

> Subjective liability, in order to be established, requires the act or harmful fact, the damage, the causal link and the agent's guilt or intent. This type of liability stems from an unlawful act or fact in which there is a damaging effect, i.e. there must be a material or moral inconvenience. There must also be fault, whether due to negligence, malpractice or recklessness, or wilful misconduct on the part of the agent. There must also be a causal link between the agent's behaviour and the actual damage. In this type of liability applied to the state, the fault or intent of the public agent or the state must be proven in order to generate the duty to indemnify or repair the damage (CAMPOS, 2011, p.88).

In the case of strict liability, the state is held responsible, regardless of fault or intent, for the damage caused by its agents, in this capacity, to third parties in an omissive or commissive manner. Regarding strict liability:

> [...] the public service did not function (omission), functioned late or functioned badly. In any of these three cases, the fault (faute) of the service or administrative accident occurs, and the state's liability arises regardless of any assessment of the employee's fault (DI PIETRO, 2009, p.642).

The state's responsibility can also be direct, which comes from the act of the person responsible, or indirect, which comes from the act of a third party linked to the agent or the fact of an animal or inanimate thing in its custody.

According to Farinelli, et.al (2011, p.61, 62, 63) there are three theories of strict liability of the state: the theory of administrative guilt, the theory of administrative risk and the theory of integral risk:

a) Administrative fault theory: the state's obligation to indemnify arises from the objective absence of the public service itself. This is not the fault of the public agent, but the special fault of the public authority, characterised by the lack of public service.

b) Administrative risk theory: the civil liability of the state for acts of commission or omission by its agents is objective in nature, i.e. there is no need to prove fault. In order to establish the objective liability of the public entity, it is enough to prove the omission and the harmful event and that this results in material or moral damage.

c) Full risk theory: the Administration is invariably responsible for the damage suffered by a third party, even if it is the result of the latter's exclusive fault, or even wilful misconduct. It is the exacerbation of the theory of administrative risk that leads to abuse and social inequity.

The Brazilian social security system requires that behaviour that flouts state rules governing its financing be curbed. Once this rule is flouted, the individual commits an illegal act. In the words of Campos:

> At the heart of state civil liability is the state's duty to make reparation for damage caused to others, due to the fault or wilful misconduct of its agents in an omissive or commissive manner, in the exercise of their functions (CAMPOS, 2011, p. 84).

The events covered by social security are events in the lives of insured people. As insured people are fragile beings, they are unable to protect their rights without the support of the state and society; if damage occurs to the insured person or their dependents, they need the protection of the state and society to help them and their families get back on their feet.

For Castro, et.al (2010, p. 167) "The active subject is the person who carries out the act described in the incriminating criminal law". The person who effectively had power of command should be held responsible.

As far as benefits are concerned, the INSS or the public office with legal personality will be the liable party; as far as funding is concerned, the liable party will be the Federal Revenue Service of Brazil. With regard to the behaviour of the INSS:

> Therefore, the INSS, as well as all local authorities, is liable to third parties with prerogatives and obligations as if it were the public administration itself. Furthermore, since it has full legal personality and holds duties and obligations, the INSS has passive legitimacy ad causam to respond judicially for its actions (FARINELI, et.al, 2011, p.102).

Once the courts have been called upon, and the interested party has been provoked, in the case of compensation for moral damage in the event of defects in the granting of benefits or in the collection of taxes, they must re-establish the legal certainty that has been shaken by the state's error.

The subjects involved in the social security legal relationship are a legal person governed by public law, responsible for the administrative acts, and an individual, the beneficiaries.

According to Farineli, et.al (2011, p. 39) "The relevant social interest of social security law in repairing damage to the insured, as well as emphasising the role of the state in solving social problems, has been proven." The social rule of law is characterised most clearly by social security.

Social security cannot fail to observe the principles that guide it, especially the principles of legality and efficiency, which guide public activity, under penalty of incurring moral damage to the insured, or to the dependent or taxpayer.

1.2. Social Security Principles

The principles and rules that govern social security and make up the 1988 constitutional system can be found in articles 194 and 195 of the Federal Constitution (CF). The general principles of law are latent principles in the legislative system, they are foundations that reconstitute successive high generalisations. Corroborating this theory:

> Constitutional principles are the foundations of the legal system and serve to guarantee a democratic state of law. As such, the principles of social security are made up of a set of programmatic rules that provide guiding objectives for the drafting of laws and a set of guarantees to be observed by the public administration in the execution of social security programmes (FARINELI, et.al, 2011, p. 33).

According to Campos (2011, p. 45), "The valorisation of principles as a transcendental form of legal sources seeks to ensure the desires of a society, at a given time, in a true and lasting way, in line with the historicity of rights".

The principles are not only applied to social security, but to its entire structure, which encompasses three segments: social security, health and social assistance.

The correct granting of social security benefits and the collection of these taxes is a fulfilment of the principles of social security. According to Balera:

> Social security aims to give everyone the protection they need. This is the content of the principle catalogued in item I of the sole paragraph of art. 194 of the Constitution. Everyone will be protected in all situations defined by law as social risks. The principle refers to both the subjects and the object of social security (BALERA, 2006, p. 157)

According to Campos (2011, p.47), "The principle of universality requires all individuals who need social support in times of need to be covered by social security".

According to Campos (2011, p.47,48), the principle of solidarity is "the most important principle because, if it were absent, it would be impossible to talk about social security. Thus, in the event of a contingency, the state, together with society, must remedy it, without any defects in the granting of social security benefits, demonstrating harmony and legal security in the system".

The principle of equality states that everyone is equal before the law from a formal point of view, and on the other hand, unequal people must be treated unequally to the extent of their inequality. In this sense:

> In this way, the granting of benefits must observe the material equality of the various social security situations in order to avoid the moral abuse of the insured or their dependents in the granting of social security benefits

and, when this occurs, to impose on the state the obligation to make reparation (CAMPOS, 2011, p.48, 49).

The principle of uniformity and equivalence of benefits and services to urban and rural populations states that "the non-granting of social security benefits to proven rural workers or the excessive requirement of proof as to their real situation, considering the precariousness of evidence of their activity in the countryside, may cause them moral distress liable to compensation." Regarding the Principle of Uniformity:

> [...] it is about giving uniform treatment to urban and rural workers, so there are identical benefits and services (uniformity) for the same events covered by the system (equivalence). This principle means, however, that there will be the same value for the benefits, since equivalence does not mean equality (CASTRO, et.al, 2010, p. 27).

The principle of selectivity and distributivity in the provision of benefits and services "distribution must be effective in the sense that the benefit is actually granted in the cases in which it should be granted." With regard to the Principle of Selectivity:

> The principle of selectivity presupposes that benefits are granted to those who actually need them, which is why Social Security must specify the requirements for granting benefits and services. In other words, a worker who has no dependents will not be granted the family allowance; someone who is temporarily unable to work due to illness will not be granted a disability pension, but sickness benefit. There is no single benefit or service, but several, which will be granted and maintained selectively, according to the person's needs (CASTRO, et.al, 2010. p. 27)

Any defect that prevents the granting of the benefit implies disobedience to the principle, and there is the possibility of compensation for the moral damage suffered. Corroborating this thesis:

> Through the first principle (selectivity), the legislator has a kind of specific mandate to study the greatest social needs in terms of social security, making it possible for these to be prioritised over others [...]. Distributivity, on the other hand, is implicit in the notion of building a free, fair and supportive society (art. 3, CF 88), as it allows us to understand that everyone should contribute according to their ability to pay and receive in

proportion to their needs (DUARTE, 2011, p.30).

According to Campos (2011, p.50), the principle of the irreducibility of the value of benefits means that "the readjustments of pensions and benefits do not, or unfairly, restore the purchasing power of these instalments, requiring the insured to seek judicial protection in order to be entitled to a real readjustment".

In this case, in addition to the material damage of not receiving what is really owed to him, it generates moral damage, due to the emotional and psychological distress it causes him. In Balera's words:

> Benefits are pecuniary instalments that cannot be modified either in their quantitative expression (monetary value) or in their qualitative expression (real value). In order to fulfil this guideline, legislation must establish the appropriate criteria for measuring the purchasing power of the benefit (BALERA, 2006 p. 21,22).

If the benefit is reduced, the value of the benefit owed must be periodically recomputed. In order for this guideline to be complied with, it is necessary for the legislation to establish the appropriate criteria for measuring the purchasing power of the benefit. If this benefit is reduced, it must be immediately restored and periodically readjusted.

The principle of equity in the form of participation in funding "refers to the need to provide for the source of funding for the creation, increase or extension of benefits and services".

The principles of social security must be respected, as failure to do so could cause moral damage to the insured, who depend on it or those who contribute to it. With regard to the principles of social security:

> The principles of social security are made up of a set of programmatic rules that provide guiding objectives for drafting laws and a set of guarantees to be observed by the public administration when implementing social security programmes (FARINELI, et.al, 2011, p. 33).

Social security is everyone's right without distinction as to race, colour or religion, and it must cater for as many risk situations as possible. Social security benefits must be granted to all who depend on them, without any defects in the concessions, otherwise the injured party must be compensated for the damage suffered.

They are important inducements for the reduction of misery and poverty in the country, since the benefits paid in cash are intended to reduce or eliminate social need and are of a food nature. In this sense:

> The defects that prevent the insured or their dependents from being granted the benefits to which they are entitled constitute an offence against their need for food and reflect on their psychological and psychic orbit, since they cause fragility to their basic vital needs, generating, as a consequence, moral damage, which must be repaired (CAMPOS, 2011, p. 78).

The principles are not only applied to social security, but to the entire structure of social security and its segments, i.e. social security, health and social assistance.

The Federal Constitution of 1988, in other words, the principles and precepts enshrined in the constitutional text, are sources of greater hierarchy and cannot be invoked as a means of resolving conflicts, but they must be respected and taken into account in the decisions that the INSS has to make with regard to insured people.

According to Balera (2006, p. 37), the amounts kept by the organisation are used to comply with what was established in the constitutive acts and social security contracts, for the benefit of society and those in need, as well as those who have been victimised by an accident.

The social security benefit is an institute personae, responsible for the existence, subsistence and survival of the human person, affecting them directly and with relevance. This thesis is corroborated:

> The purpose of social security benefits (benefits paid in cash) is to reduce or eliminate the state of social need. Social security benefits are the basic social security needs provided for in the Brazilian social security system (FARINELI, et.al, 2011, p. 40).

In social security law, there are two sides: the beneficiaries and taxpayers are the victims, and the institutions that manage social protection are the victims. However, damage can occur to legal entities and even state management bodies, which can be victims of attacks when they occur.

Compensation for moral damages on the one hand comforts the offended party and on the other punishes the offender, constituting a measure aimed at preventing further damage to third parties by public services:

> If social security moral damage, with the condemnation of those truly guilty, does not serve to improve public services, it will be reduced to a fad or a source of extra income for the unscrupulous (MARTINEZ, 2005, p.23, 24).

According to Henk (2012, p. 311) "The obligation to pay moral damages will fulfil its purpose, because in the regressive action, it will induce the public agent to deal with a fundamental right in order to safeguard the dignity of the human person, achieving efficiency."

As for the insured, he will have a bonus in addition to the benefits to which he is entitled. They won't recover the moral damage, but they will alleviate it. In this context, liability for moral damage in social security law is appropriate, due to the offence against dignity.

It can be concluded that the condemnation of moral damages to offenders should serve to improve public services, which should aim to protect society and maintain human dignity.

2. APPLICATION OF MORAL DAMAGE TO SOCIAL SECURITY BENEFITS

There are various reasons for the undue cancellation of benefits, such as administrative errors (homonyms), improper medical examinations and suspicions of fraud in the granting of benefits.

In these cases, the feelings of humiliation, indignation, deprivation and powerlessness experienced by those who have been harmed by the Social Security Agency are common. With regard to moral damage:

> The conceptualisation of moral damage being clear, it is evident that it has a massive impact on social security relations. Every day, thousands of insured people have their applications for benefits denied by the INSS. Of this universe of denials, forensic practice shows that many benefits should be granted (FARINELI, et.al, 2011, p. 114).

Compensation for moral damage in the event of defects in the granting of social security benefits is the obligation of the State, since it must take care to grant benefits without defects and demand the correct contribution. In this sense:

> Thus, "restitution is resolved in the sacrifice of an identical interest, while punishment is resolved in the sacrifice of a different interest to be punished according to the precept, correlatively, restitution has the character of satisfaction, while punishment has the character of affliction". (CAHALI, 1999, p. 38)

In the same way, appeals bodies have an obligation to repress defects in the granting of social security benefits, under penalty of generating moral damage subject to reparation.

In this case, the Judiciary, once provoked by the interested party, must impose moral reparation in the event of damage to insured persons and taxpayers, in order to re-establish the legal certainty that has been shaken.

The INSS has frequently denied undeniable rights in an abusive and arbitrary manner through its medical experts. People who are ill and unable to work receive hasty medical discharges, even though they are unable to return to work. According to Campos:

> On the other hand, when the INSS or the Federal Government repeatedly commits unlawful acts, the amount of moral damage should be set at a punitive level, gradually increasing in proportion to the recurrence of harmful behaviour (CAMPOS, 2011, p. 118).

The unjust denial of a social security benefit results in the unjust deprivation of food, which is essential to the insured person's subsistence. Compensation must take into account the fact that the insured person has been contributing for years and when he needs it most, his benefit is unjustly denied.

Flaws arising from non-compliance with the rules in the administrative process for granting social security benefits can cause moral damage to the insured, and compensation is required. In the words of Henk:

> In this context, the defect that makes it impossible to access or maintain the social security benefit can affect not only the property sphere, but also the off-balance sheet sphere, hurting the dignity of their existence by preventing the possibility of self-determination. In this situation, merely restoring or granting the benefit due is not enough, and compensation for moral damages should be considered (HENK, 2012, p. 289).

The social security administrative process must guarantee all insured people and their dependents due process of law, with no surprises for the beneficiaries, so that they can exercise their rights.

According to Campos (2011 p. 95), this is why the administrative process must follow the principles that inform it, in order to allow for adequate coverage of social risks, without further damage to the beneficiaries.

2.1 Social Security Benefits

The benefits included in the General Social Security System are expressed in benefits and services. Benefits and services are provided for in the social security system and guarantee the basic needs of the insured. Corroborating this thesis:

> Benefits are a genus, of which benefits and services are species. Benefits are amounts paid in cash to insured people and their dependents. Services are assistance and support provided by Social Security to beneficiaries in general, to the extent that local conditions and resources allow. The purpose of social security benefits (benefits paid in cash) is to reduce or eliminate the state of social need, and they are of a food nature (FARINELI, et.al, 2011, p.40).

According to Duarte (2011, p. 213), "Retirement is the social security benefit for excellence, together with the pension for death. Both permanently replace the insured person's income and ensure their subsistence."

According to Campos (2011, p.66), disability pensions are paid to insured people with health problems that permanently prevent them from working.

Old-age retirement will be granted on reaching the age of 65 if a man and 60 if a woman, once the qualifying period of 180 monthly contributions has been fulfilled. In this context:

> Age retirement is a benefit granted on account of the insured person's advanced age and fulfilment of the waiting period, which is 180 monthly contributions and 65 years of age for men and 60 for women (FARINELI, et.al, 2011, p. 41).

Retirement for contribution time is granted to the insured person who has completed 30 years or more of contribution if they are a woman, and 35 years or more if they are a man, while compulsory retirement is granted due to the insured person's advanced age (70 years of age if they are a man and 65 years of age if they are a woman). According to this theory:

> The value of the monthly retirement benefit for contribution time is calculated in the same way as the monthly benefit income for age retirement, i.e. by the simple arithmetic average of the highest contribution salaries corresponding to eighty per cent of the entire contribution period, multiplied by the social security factor (CAMPOS, 2011, p. 68).

Special retirement is granted to those who work in conditions harmful to the health or integrity of the insured, with a waiting period of 180 contributions and a minimum of 15, 20 or 25 years of exposure to harmful activities.

Sickness benefit is paid to insured persons who are unable to carry out their labour activities for more than 15 days. According to this theory:

> The inability to work or perform one's usual activity for more than fifteen consecutive days: the inability required in this case is, as a rule, temporary (either partial or total) and not permanent and total, as required for the granting of a disability pension (DUARTE, 2011, p. 297,298)

Prison benefit is payable to the dependant of an insured person who is employed on a low income and who is in prison. Even if the employer chooses to terminate the contract without just cause, the dependants of the insured person will be entitled to the benefit.

Accident benefit is the result of the consequences of accidents suffered, such as accidents at work or work-related illnesses. This benefit is granted the day after the sickness benefit ceases, regardless of the employee's pay.

A death pension is a benefit paid to the dependents of an insured person who dies, whether they are retired or not. In this sense:

> The death pension is a benefit paid to the dependents of an insured man or woman who dies, whether retired or not, as expressly provided for in art. 201, V of the Federal Constitution, regulated by art. 74 of the RGPS Law. This is an ongoing payment that replaces the deceased insured person's remuneration. In view of this, it is considered an inalienable right of the beneficiaries who are entitled to it (CASTRO, et.al, 2010, p. 237)

Maternity pay is granted to pregnant workers for a period of 120 days, starting 28 (twenty-eight) days before childbirth and ending 91 (ninety-one) days after, including the day of childbirth.

The family wage is a monthly benefit paid to low-income workers who are employees or self-employed, according to the number of children they have up to the age of 14. With regard to the family wage:

> The benefit is paid by quota for each child aged 14 or under. If the father and mother are insured employees, they are both entitled to the family allowance. In order to receive the benefit, the insured person will need to show the child's birth certificate or adoption judgement, the vaccination booklet or equivalent for children under the age of 7 and proof of school attendance if the dependent is over the age of 7 (FARINELI, et.al, 2011, p. 42).

Welfare benefit for the elderly and disabled - LOAS, this benefit is provided for in Article 203, V of the Federal Constitution, and is due to the elderly or disabled people who prove they do not have the means to provide for their own subsistence.

So these are the social security benefits that are subject to compensation for moral damage if they are wrongly denied by the INSS or defrauded, because it is through the relationship between the insured and the Autarchy that support for beneficiaries is possible and if it is wrongly denied the insured will be in a situation of social need, due to the impossibility of obtaining their own subsistence.

2.2 Flaws that give rise to moral damages in social security benefits

2.2.1 Cancellation or denial of benefits

The INSS's liability is objective, i.e. it depends on the existence of conduct, damage and a causal link. When an insured person who is temporarily unable to work is wrongly denied an extension of their benefit by the medical examination, they must be compensated in court. Along the same lines:

> The rejection by the Social Security Authority of a benefit application, when the applicant fulfils all the legal requirements, is an unlawful act and can be challenged in court, as it is an injury to a right (CASTRO, et.al, 2010, p. 196).

If the decision is reformed administratively or judicially, it is up to the injured party to file a lawsuit for compensation for the material damage suffered. In this sense:

> [...] If the decision is not reformed administratively or judicially, and the benefit is thus reinstated with retroactive effect, the injured party will have to go to court to claim compensation for the material damage they have suffered, which will be equivalent to the benefit wages they no longer

receive due to the expert error, and the plaintiff will have the burden of proving that the benefit was due during the period claimed (FARINELI, et.al, 2011, p. 111,112).

More serious and clear are the moral damages suffered by those who receive a benefit and have it unduly cancelled by the INSS, since the INSS can carry out reviews of benefits that have already been granted and prevent fraud, and can cancel the benefit granted as long as there is proof of the irregularity, human dignity is shaken by directly affecting self-determination. Corroborating this thesis:

> One example is the person who, despite being unable to work, has their benefit refused or terminated, and is exposed to surviving on the charity of others or begging, or to returning to or staying in work. This situation is akin to subjecting the insured to forced labour, since being incapacitated means having no capacity, and working in this condition is forcing the person to do something they cannot bear (HENK, 2012, p. 291).

In cases where the cancellation or rejection of the benefit is unfair, this is a case of moral damage, and there is no need to prove damages. This is what we are told:

> [...] the incidence of immaterial damage occurs when, unjustly, an INSS insured person fails to receive a maintenance payment due to him, leaving him without a much more valuable asset than credit, his monthly income, essential for his subsistence and maintenance of his dignity (FARINELI, et.al, 2011, p. 117).

Case law also takes the view that the damage must be repaired: ADMINISTRATIVE. INDEMNITY ACTION. MORAL DAMAGES. CANCELLATION OF SOCIAL SECURITY BENEFIT. AMOUNT OF COMPENSATION. PREQUESTIONING.

> 1. The jurisprudence of the Superior Court of Justice has consolidated in the sense that, in the modern concept of compensation for moral damage, the agent's liability prevails by virtue of the mere fact of the violation, so that proof of actual damage is unnecessary, unlike what happens with material damage.
>
> 2. With regard to setting the amount of compensation, with due regard for the principles of reasonableness and proportionality, it

must fulfil the purpose of compensation and prevention: compensating the affected party for the damage suffered and pedagogically preventing similar acts from occurring again.

3. The prequestioning claim is accepted in order to avoid the inadmissibility of appeals to higher courts arising exclusively from the lack of express mention of the provisions considered by the party to have been violated, which have been implicitly considered in the judgement, as they are pertinent to the matter decided.[2]

According to Farineli, et.al (2011, p. 101) "In the administrative process for granting, extending or cancelling benefits, the social security system must be taken into account." In the event of doubt, the INSS must decide in favour of the insured.

Therefore, it is necessary to check whether the cancellation of the benefit was due or not. If the cancellation was due and if the insured person was given the opportunity to defend himself fully, the INSS is justified; if the cancellation was undue, the INSS has a duty to compensate the insured person for the damage caused.

The moral damage caused by the refusal of social security benefits stems from the objective civil liability of the INSS, which can be condemned regardless of the presence of intent or guilt. However, it is not every denial that generates moral damage, but only those in which it is proven that, even if there is incapacity and serious illness, there is an unjustified refusal by the Social Security to grant it and that this act causes negative repercussions in the life of the insured.

The INSS will cancel the benefit in cases where there is no defence, or when the defence is unfounded, or when the evidence presented is insufficient, and the beneficiary will be notified and will have the right to appeal.

Compensation for moral damages must comfort the indemnified party for the unjust damage experienced, compensating for the afflictions suffered with an amount that brings consolation. With regard to compensation for moral damage:

---

[2] Judgement, Class: AC - APELAÇÃO CIVEL, Case: 2007.72.04.001208-7 UF: SC Date of Decision: 09/02/2010 Judging Body: THIRD COURT, Entire Content: View Full Text Citation: View Citation, Source D.E. 03/03/2010, Rapporteur NICOLAU KONKEL JÚNIOR

> It is primarily a question of making the injured party's assets - the common guarantee of creditors - liable for the damaging effects experienced by the injured party, restoring the parties to their previous state (BITTAR, 1997, p. 25).

It is also important for the injured party to restore their personal situation, or at least to minimise the effects of the damage they have suffered. It is important to attribute the negative effects of their actions to the offender, in order to maintain social tranquillity.

2.2.2. Suspension of Benefits

The beneficiary applies for the benefit at the INSS, and the application is carefully analysed. If it coincides with the dictates of the law, the benefit is granted. Later, by force of law or by binding act, the grant may be reviewed. With regard to the suspension of benefits:

> If bad faith, collusion, simulation, ideological falsehood, fraud or impropriety are present, the monthly payments are suspended and, in extreme cases, if exhaustion and non-existence of the right are proven, the benefit is cancelled in compliance with STF Precedent 473 (MARTINEZ, 2005, p. 181).

Suspension is only applicable when there is no damage to the person concerned and its duration will depend on proof by the person entitled to it to prove their right, while when the benefit is cancelled it is the definitive extinction of the benefit.

In both cases, the due process of law must be observed until the end of the process, with a final and unappealable judgement.

Both suspension and cancellation are drastic solutions that can harm human rights, and can only be taken if there is certainty that the right is inappropriate. In this sense:

> In social insurance legislation, there are certain situations that authorise the INSS to stop paying the benefit, suspending the benefit due. However, this situation should not be confused with the cancellation of the benefit: in suspension, the benefit has only had its payment suspended; in cancellation, the INSS terminates its obligation to pay the beneficiary (CASTRO, et.al, 2010, p. 196).

According to case law from the Federal Regional Court (TRF), this is also the case with regard to the suspension of benefits:

NECESSARY REMITTANCE AND CIVIL APPEAL. UNDUE SUSPENSION OF BENEFIT. NON-EXISTENT DEATH. ERRONEOUS COMMUNICATION FROM THE REGISTRY OFFICE. QUICK SOLUTION. DELAY IN PAYMENT OF ONLY 04 DAYS. MORAL DAMAGES, UNCHARACTERISED. MERE ANNOYANCE. INDEMNIFICATION. DISABLED.

NECESSARY REMITTANCE AND APPEAL UPHELD. 1) Social security benefit unduly suspended due to erroneous indication of the insured's death. 2) Rapid administrative solution, resulting in a delay in payment of the benefit of only four days. 3) No injury to the insured's personality capable of giving rise to a duty to indemnify on the part of the Autarchy. (4) The occurrence of a fault in the INSS's computerised system, which was, to a certain extent, neutralised by the Authority's rapid response in resolving the problem, correcting the situation in four days, without any further damage to the insured, characterising mere annoyance, incapable of generating the obligation to compensate the Plaintiff for moral damages. 5. remittitur and appeal granted, to dismiss the initial claims and order the plaintiff to pay attorney's fees, set at 10% of the value of the case, in accordance with Article 20, paragraph 4, of the CPC, with the order being subject to the terms of Law 1,060/1950. 3

The reinstatement of a suspended benefit can occur because the insured person's right has been recognised or because they have presented new evidence, in which case the granting body is not at fault. However, in the case of recognition of the insured's right, this characterises an error on the part of the administration, in which case moral reparation is due.

2.2.3. Late concession and uncollected social contributions

Public administrations have a bad reputation for being slow to fulfil their obligations. When it comes to insurance benefits, a delay in granting them causes damage to the insured.

[3] Acórdão, Origem: TRF-2, Classe: AC - APELAÇÃO CÍVEL - 593774, Processo: 200951018124368 UF: RJ Orgão Julgador: SEGUNDA TURMA ESPECIALIZADA, Data Decisão: 12/12/2013 Documento: TRF-200286646 Fonte, E-DJF2R - Data: 17/01/2014, Reporting Judge, Federal Judge MESSOD AZULAY NETO Reporting Judge, Federal Judge MARCELO PEREIRA DA SILVA, Voting Members, ANDRÉ FONTES MARCELO PEREIRA DA SILVA

The legislation also does not stipulate the time for public offices to attend to the insured.

However, according to Provisional Measure No. 316 of 11 August 2006, converted into Law No. 11.430/2006, it revoked the provision of Law No. 8.213/91, adding Article 41-A, paragraph 5:

> The first payment of the benefit will be made no later than forty-five days after the date on which the insured presents the documentation required for it to be granted (wording given by Law No. 11.665 of 2008)

The legislator has ordered the monthly payments in arrears to be corrected, and this is not a legal favour, since the correction is a simple updating of the currency and not a punishment. The measure inhibits delays and acts as a sanctioning rule, since delays in granting benefits cause suffering for the insured.

All that remains for the insured is material compensation, which is the granting of the benefit plus currency correction and interest on arrears, and if necessary, moral compensation when the claim of those who are entitled to it is not met and they can prove it.

With regard to uncollected social contributions, the taxpayer is not always the subject of the obligation to pay the contributions; there are cases in which the responsibility lies with a third party, who is responsible for the correct collection and delivery of the amount due, and who is subject to criminal and administrative sanctions in the event of non-compliance with the obligation. With regard to the collection of contributions:

> [...] if a company does not deduct from its employees' pay the social security contributions that they must pay, and consequently does not pay them to the Social Security Authority, the latter, upon observing the illegal conduct, will, through inspection, demand the contributions no longer from the employees, but from the employer, who is responsible for complying with the legal obligation (CASTRO, et.al, 2010, p. 124).

Employers' contributions are levied on payroll and other labour income, turnover and profit, while workers contribute on the basis of remuneration or production. Any misappropriation of funds from the contribution is an affront to the destination of these amounts.

2.2.4. Equivocal Expertise

The insured person, the person dependent on the benefit, has to undergo a medical examination, the documents are examined by doctors who are often not specialised in the area, and the examination is quick, and in the overwhelming majority of cases the benefits are denied.

It is common practice for the INSS to unduly delay the payment of benefits. This attitude often goes beyond its obligation to pay the arrears, and the family's moral damage must also be compensated. Because of this, the INSS can be held civilly liable for making a serious error in assessing the incapacity of workers, which is often easily recognisable by any doctor.

When comparing the statements made by private professionals and the decisions of administrative and judicial experts, medical mistakes are made. The damage caused to those who are ill or unable to work is very great, even worse if the person is unemployed. In this context:

> The medical expert's error causes damage to the protected party and, when confirmed definitively, is a prerequisite for an action to compensate for moral damage. Which, of course, will never redeem them from all the suffering, anguish and humiliation they have gone through (MARTINEZ, 2005, p. 155).

In the view of Farineli, et.al (2011, p. 117) "expert medical error causes damage to the protected party and, when confirmed, definitively, is a prerequisite for an action to compensate for moral damage".

With regard to medical error, the case law of the Federal Court of Appeals (TRF) is unequivocal as to its reparation:

> ADMINISTRATIVE - CIVIL LIABILITY OF THE STATE - MEDICAL ERROR - ADSTRUCTION TO THE REQUEST - PERIODIC DAMAGES - BUDGET - FIXATION I - The Federal University of Rio de Janeiro cannot be held responsible for the damages that the plaintiff claims to have suffered when, in a hospital accredited by the social security authority, a substance was inoculated into her body that caused an allergic reaction. The plaintiff's fall on the premises of the university hospital where she worked is not directly related to the poor care provided in the public network, which is why the decision rejecting UFRJ's claim was correct. II - The INSS's appeal should not be upheld, since, as the judgement rightly pointed out, "the substance that caused the damage was administered by an IBIC agent, during the performance of the service it had undertaken to provide to the INSS (then INPS), as can be seen from the contract on pages 24/26". The terms of the aforementioned agreement show that the former INPS contracted with IBIC to perform medical services in favour of victims of accidents at work, and that the municipality should be held responsible for any damage caused to injured patients by the conduct of its chosen agent. III - The appellate claim to cumulate the condemnation related to moral damages with the determination of pension and physical damages lacks correlation with the delimitation of the dispute established based on the request deduced in the initial petition, which reaches exclusively: "by way of reparation, to mitigate his pain, the amount that is arbitrated, in view of the damage suffered by his health, his psychic" (fl. 05). Reparation established to "alleviate the pain", in view of the "psychological damage", refers to the so-called moral damage, and it is not lawful for the appellant, on appeal, to seek to broaden the scope of the claim, in subversion of the adversarial

process and, ultimately, due process of law. IV - As for the amount arbitrated, there really was a mismatch with the case law of the Superior Court of Justice which, in cases of serious medical error, has established amounts corresponding to double what was established in the judgement. In fact, the expert report showed that the plaintiff has had to live with constant headaches, as well as dizziness and visual disturbances, due to the existence of the remains of LIPIODOL contrast lodged at the base of her brain, without modern medicine knowing of a technique that allows the removal of said residues. This shows that the damage suffered by the appellant as a result of medical error is permanent. The consequences of the negligent behaviour of the public doctors must therefore be reduced by means of adequate pecuniary compensation, which I set at one hundred thousand reais, an amount to be subject to monetary restatement (JF calculation manual) and interest of 1% per month from the present date. V - INSS appeal and remittance dismissed. Plaintiff's appeal upheld in part.[3]

The purpose of compensation for moral damage is to comfort the injured party for the damage suffered, thus alleviating their anguish and distress with an amount that brings them comfort.

Compensation for moral damage must take into account that the reduction in the assets of the agent who caused the damage discourages other similar practices. Compensation must be more rigorous when the agent causing the damage is a repeat offender, as is the case with the INSS. With regard to compensation for moral damage to the insured:

> [...] the social security agency is a true arm of the Federal Public Administration and, as such, enjoys enormous financial power. On the other hand, there are endless possibilities for its activities to cause extremely serious damage to insured people (FARINELI, et.al, 2011, p.

---

[3] Acórdão, Origem: TRF-2, Classe: AC - APELAÇÃO CÍVEL - 265004, Processo: 200102010182860 UF: RJ Orgão Julgador: QUINTA TURMA ESPECIALIZADA, Data Decisão: 07/05/2008, Documento: TRF-200184077, Relator, Desembargador Federal MAURO LUIS ROCHA LOPES, Votantes, PAULO ESPIRITO SANTO, ANTONIO CRUZ NETTO, VERA LUCIA LIMA, MAURO LUIS ROCHA LOPES

118).

The amount of compensation must be observed on a case-by-case basis, taking into account the extent of the damage and the offender's purchasing power, thus fulfilling the reparatory functions of compensation.

2.2.5. Inattentive Service and Lack of Guidance

Poor customer service can be defined as a lack of urbanity, politeness and promptness on the part of those who have an obligation to serve the public. It often occurs in Social Security agencies, and most of the time this discourtesy happens to the elderly. Corroborating this thesis:

> It comes with indolence, disrespect and rude treatment. Sometimes this is aggravated by carelessness, negligence and inattention to the rights, interests and documents of the person concerned. Unfortunately, this is not so uncommon in public administration and can be explained by the federal government's terrible human resources policy and its deep institutional contempt for the civil servant, lack of awareness of their social role and a certain amount of mistrust (MARTINEZ, 2005, p.136).

As a result, there have been many lawsuits for moral damages, because poor service offends citizenship, as the attendants forget to observe the urbanity and politeness that should be shown to the public, for which people need to be well trained and compensated.

The case law of the Federal Court of Appeal is peaceful with regard to the offence against the insured: ADMINISTRATIVE. CIVIL LIABILITY. OFFENCE AGAINST PERSONALITY RIGHTS. INSS BENEFICIARY

> OFFENDED BY A SOCIAL SECURITY AGENT AT THE INSS POST IN ITAGUAÍ (RJ). "BLACK AND DUMB". REVERSAL OF THE BURDEN OF PROOF. (1) INSS beneficiary offended at the Itaboraí post, being called, among other offences, "black and dumb". 2) Inversion of the burden of proof decreed, in view of the appellant's flagrant procedural hyposufficiency. Valuation of the

evidence made more flexible, given the initial evidence of the allegations, consisting of a witness and a written complaint, on the date of the incident, addressed to the Head of the Post. (3) It would be diabolical evidence to require the appellant to prove the alleged right by the testimony of INSS employees, who have no interest in having the facts clarified. However, the testimonies were to the effect that there had been an altercation on the premises of the Post, followed by the appellant's indignation at having been offended. 4 - For moral damage to be established, proof of the harmful event is sufficient. The humiliation and vexation experienced cannot be assessed or proven, as they are subjective. 5) Appeal upheld to reverse the first degree judgement and order the INSS to pay R$ 10,000.00.[5]

Proving the fact is onerous, as there are no written records, only the offended party can use testimonial evidence that they witnessed the event, as well as media reports. Moral damage is only evidenced in more serious cases such as swearing or obvious mistreatment. In Cahali's view:

> Thus, although some case law questions the need for proof of even moral damage, it is from the perspective of the subjective element of the offender's conduct that the issue offers greater significance (CAHALI, 1999, p. 306)

For the judge who has to hear a case like this, he or she will have to be intellectually and professionally calm, know the routine of these cases, and detect whether it was a moment of folly or profound disrespect for taxpayers.

Public offices have a duty to provide good guidance to those concerned, informing them of their rights and clarifying them in the best possible way. Lack of guidance, which is almost always verbal, by its very nature is difficult to ascertain, but when it is, it can lead to lawsuits for moral damage. Along the same lines:

> It is the responsibility of government bodies to provide any and all information necessary for the proper fulfilment of the CNPS's competences, including technical studies; and to send the CNPS, at least

> two months before it is sent to the National Congress, the Social Security budget proposal, duly detailed (CAsTRO, et.al, 2010, p. 19).

In the majority of cases, the lack of guidance is seen as an administrative failure that justifies political action, and not actions for moral damages, unless the error is documented in a booklet or written information, otherwise guilt will rarely be proven, as the service is provided at information desks.

2.2.6. Calculation Error and Presumption of Fraud

The social security benefits due are calculated manually or using computer resources. As such, they are subject to errors in their calculation. In this case, the value of the benefits may be lower than due or higher, and this erroneous payment over a long period of time can cause damage to the insured.

The insured person having to pay back what they thought was theirs and spending some time suffering from this deduction can be as distressing as having to wait to be paid what they are owed.

It is an easy task to estimate the amount of the error if it is against the insured, paying them the arrears of the difference plus interest on arrears, but if the insured has to return what was wrongly received, it becomes difficult and can be settled with moral compensation. As for moral compensation:

> [...] the State is responsible for making reparation for judicial error, and the compensation must cover the moral and material damages resulting from the execution of the condemnatory sentence, to the detriment of the offended party, all the more so when it is proven that the error was not due to an act or fault attributable to the accused and that the accusation was public (CAHALI, 1999, p. 682).

Fraud attempts and consummation are commonplace, with many insured people obtaining benefits that were maintained until their death and in some cases received after their death, without this ever being discovered.

With regard to fraud in relation to social security benefits, there is case law from the Federal Supreme Court (STF):

> REVIDENTIAL. REINSTATEMENT OF BENEFIT SUSPENDED ON SUSPICION OF FRAUD. REGULARITY OF THE BENEFIT PROVEN. INDEMNITY FOR MORAL DAMAGE. I - The Administration must carry out a wide-ranging and binding activity in order to ascertain, through a regular administrative process, the exact fulfilment of all the elements for granting the benefit, with a view to seeking the material truth. The practice so common within the INSS of reviewing the granting act based on the mere silence of the insured, or on consulting the CNIS, is not admissible, since it must be based on the inarguable premise of the existence of a previous administrative procedure, which would have resulted in the act granting the benefit, which enjoys the presumption of veracity. II - The absence of records referring to employment relationships prior to the creation of the CNIS, in itself, cannot be considered a suspicion of irregularity in the granting of the benefit. III - In such cases, it is necessary for the Autarchy to take steps to prove the irregularity of the employment relationship used to grant the benefit or to supplement the CNIS data with other strong indications of irregularities. IV - In the present case, the court was right to note that the data obtained from the CNIS is often flawed, untrue, as in the present case, given that, in fact, the document on page 90, obtained from the JUCERJA database, the body responsible for registering the activities of companies in this state, the company O. DIAS DA SILVA ALFAIATE started its activities on 01.12.1965, and not on 10/02/1972, as erroneously stated in the CNIS, so it is possible that the plaintiff did have an employment contract with the company between 05.12.1967 and 30.04.1971. And, as the document on page 88 informs us, the plaintiff has been registered with the PIS since January 1971, i.e. he was registered with the Social Security system during the term of the aforementioned employment contract, and it is also a relevant fact that the annotations made on his work cards are in perfect chronological order, have characteristics of the time and there is no evidence of any defect or erasure on them (pages 23/45), and it is therefore necessary to recognise the veracity of the employment relationship in question. V - The speciality of the work carried out by the plaintiff at CIA. BRASILEIRA DE DISTRIBUIÇÃO PÃO DE AÇÚCAR from 24.08.1983 to 01.10.1997 must also be recognised in view of the information contained in SB-40 on page 19 (already presented in the administrative concession process, according to the copy

attached on page 120), according to which the plaintiff/appellant, during that period, worked for the aforementioned company as a Boner and in charge of the company's Butchery Section, exposed to the noxious agent cold, on a regular basis. VI - In this case, it can be inferred that the requirement to prove effective exposure to harmful agents established in Paragraph 4 of Article 57 and Paragraphs 1 and 2 of Article 58 of Law No. 8,213/91, as amended, respectively, by Laws Nos. 9,032/95 and 9,528/97, can only be applied to the time of service rendered during its validity, and not retroactively, as it is a restrictive condition for recognition. VII - There is no doubt that the plaintiff suffered severe distress when his social security benefit was unduly cancelled for more than a year (since the cancellation occurred in May 2011), as well as when he was indicted in the criminal sphere on suspicion of fraud. In this case, there is no doubt that the distress suffered goes beyond mere dissatisfaction, and there is an offence to dignity. VIII - Appeal and remittitur dismissed.[4]

Faced with the various possibilities of fraud, ranging from simulating a non-existent relationship, lying or even falsifying documents. Many insured people have had their benefits granted and maintained until their death and in some cases even after their death.

For the internal affairs department, it is difficult to carry out an exhaustive investigation into fraud, with only allegations of suspicion arising, or at most what may be happening is an irregularity that can be remedied or not. This thesis is supported:

> Faced with the infinite number of hypotheses, ranging from the simulation of a non-existent relationship, a simple lie to gross or technically perfect forgery, it will never be possible to establish general rules (MARTINEZ, 2005, p. 163).

If the allegation of fraud is not proven, it can lead to an attack on morals, since saying that someone is a fraudster is a very serious matter, and if it is proven that there

---

[4] Acórdão, Origem: TRF-2 Classe: APELREEX - APELAÇÃO / REEXAME NECESSÁRIO - 579464, Processo: 201151018082435 UF: RJ, Orgão Julgador: SEGUNDA TURMA ESPECIALIZADA, Data Decisão: 26/06/2013 Document: TRF-200278932, Rapporteur, Federal Judge MESSOD AZULAY NETO, Voting Members, THEOPHILO MIGUEL, ANDRÉ FONTES, MESSOD AZULAY NETO, MARCELO PEREIRA DA SILVA

was no fraud, the attack is characterised and can be repaired.

If the benefit has been cancelled or suspended, there will be material and moral damage to the beneficiary subject to reparation. If fraud is found, it must be severely punished, with the offender having to make good what they have illegally obtained.

2.2.7. Slow Review of Benefits and Transparency in Complementation

The most common cases brought before the federal courts against the social security system are those for the revision of calculations against the rejection of the granting and incorporation of benefits.

In these cases, a request for a revision of the calculation only depends on internal bureaucratic measures, so if there is a delay in revising these calculations, it is the sole fault of the Public Administration.

If the insured person files a lawsuit asking for the calculation to be revised and is successful, in addition to the monthly instalments and allowances in arrears, they will be entitled to the additional amount earned as part of their regular monthly income.

Once the unjustified delay has been characterised, there is property damage to be repaired, as well as moral damage. Proof of the delay is characterised by the filing of the request and the letter granting the calculation, so moral damage is evident.

With regard to the Administration's liability for damages to the agent, case law observes that:

> CONSTITUTIONAL AND ADMINISTRATIVE LAW. LIABILITY FOR PUBLIC ADMINISTRATION DAMAGES. FAULT OF THE AGENT. LACK OF SERVICE. I - Despite the provisions of paragraph 6 of article 37 of the Constitution of the Republic, the liability of a state body for damage caused by the omission of one of its agents must be analysed subjectively, insofar as the omission of the body only conditioned the occurrence of the harmful event, with the omission of the public agent as the true cause (art. 15 of the Civil Code). III - In the field of moral damage, although there is no consensus in the legal world as to the requirements for its perfect configuration, it is notorious that mere misfortunes or everyday annoyances cannot

serve as grounds for such a claim, otherwise the very mens legis of art. 5, V and X of the constitutional text would be disfigured, and a loophole would be opened for the cascading condemnation of millionaire indemnities. III - Once the damage experienced has been proven through witness evidence, the causal link, albeit in a less robust manner, and the omission in the provision of the public service, an omission attributed to the administrative agent, characterising a lack of service, it is the duty of the Public Administration to compensate. IV - Appeal dismissed.[5]

Article 202, paragraph 1 of the Federal Constitution, as amended, states Constitutional No. 20/98 that:

> The complementary law referred to in this article will ensure that participants in the benefit plans of private pension organisations have full access to information regarding the management of their respective plans (CF, 1988).

All information that is pertinent to the beneficiary's interest, with the exception of information protected by privacy, must be provided. Information must be made available to beneficiaries, in the forms and within the time limits established by the regulatory and supervisory body, when requested. Article 5, XXXII of the Federal Constitution states that:

> Everyone has the right to receive from public bodies information of their private interest, or of collective or general interest, which will be provided within the time limit of the law, under penalty of liability, except for those whose secrecy is essential to the security of society and the State (CF, 1998).

Article 5, XIV of the Federal Constitution also states that: "everyone is guaranteed access to information and the secrecy of the source is safeguarded, when necessary for professional practice".

Any acts that offend transparency must be inhibited by collective measures, obliging the manager to widely publicise the information that has been withheld. If the

---

[5] 199902010478271 - CIVIL APPEAL DATE OF DECISION: 30/10/2002 DATE OF PUBLICATION: 24/02/2003 RAPPORTEUR: ANDRÉ FONTES DIREITO

information that has been withheld causes damage to the beneficiary, moral reparation is due.

2.2.8. Withholding Documents and Refusal of Protocol and Loss of Process

The documents of beneficiaries or taxpayers are their property and cannot be seized by anyone, unless they are proof of an offence.

The social security agencies are able to examine the documents of beneficiaries in order to grant or not grant benefits, but once they have been analysed they must be returned. Along the same lines:

> The unreasonable retention of documents is improper and harmful to the citizen, causing damage to be assessed in each circumstance, justifying the pursuit of compensation in the moral sphere (MARTINEZ, 2005, p. 145).

Those who receive the documents receive them on a temporary basis, and are allowed to microfilm, photograph and make copies of them. They can also authenticate them, but on a temporary basis, and can never retain any of the insured's personal documents.

The filing of claims is a citizen's right; in the case of social security, unlike the judiciary, and because the claimant is considered to be underprivileged, their claims must be accepted, even without a previous legal claim. With regard to filing applications:

> Filing a request, whatever it may be, is a constitutional right. It can be a wish put forward to the public or private administration, an ordinary wish that is of great importance to the applicant, who has made their claim there (however simple it may be) (MARTINEZ, 2005, p. 142).

In general, the staff at the filing counter think that if the applicant has no right, then there is no need to file the application.

The person who receives a request has every right to reject it if it is not characterised according to the rules in force, but they can never refuse to file it. The person who receives the request must respond to the request and give reasons for the rejection, otherwise the principle of full defence and adversarial proceedings will be offended. In this sense:

> However, the INSS cannot do without respecting the fundamental rights to an adversarial proceeding and a full defence, which are mandatory in any judicial or administrative procedure (Constitution, art. 5). Seen from this angle, paragraph 6 of article 179 of the Regulation is unconstitutional, as it aims to authorise the INSS to suspend benefits arbitrarily, without there being any reasonable evidence of illegality (CASTRO, et.al, 2010, p. 197,198).

According to Article 5, XIV, of the Federal Constitution, everyone has the right to information, and according to Article 5, XXXIII, of the Federal Constitution, public bodies are obliged to provide information, and everyone has the right to petition public authorities in defence of their rights, Article 5, XXXIV, a, and to obtain certificates, Article 5, XXXIV, b, of the Federal Constitution.

One of the main arguments used for refusing the protocol is that the applicant does not meet the conditions or does not have the documents to prove that they are entitled to the request.

However, according to article 105 of the PBPS: "The presentation of incomplete documentation does not constitute grounds for refusing a benefit application". And the attendants are aware of this article, meaning that it is not for lack of knowledge that the application is refused.

It is very important for the claimant to have his request for a protocol granted, because the payment of a due instalment can be paid from the date of the protocol, failing which the claimant will be compensated for property damage and will be assessed as to whether or not there is moral damage.

The material evidence that accompanies an application can be decisive in recognising a citizen's right. According to Martinez (2005, p. 140) "a technical report issued in the past, a certificate of length of service, a military certificate, are of enormous importance for the insured person to prove length of service".

If the annotations filed with the Administration are lost, the insured may not be granted a benefit if a certain document is missing, thus causing great damage to the insured. In Bittar's view:

> It is therefore understandable that any unjust damage suffered by a person should find a response in the legal system, since, given the unity of the theory of damage, it is directed, at the level of the Law, towards the full satisfaction of violated interests (BITTAR, 1997, p.38).

The case law of the Federal Court of Justice states that administrative proceedings are lost:

> CIVIL LIABILITY - INSS - MISSING OF ADMINISTRATIVE PROCEEDINGS FOR REVIEW OF PENSION BENEFIT - MATERIAL DAMAGE NOT SPECIFIED - MORAL DAMAGE CONFIGURED. 1. After the appellant won an administrative proceeding for review of his pension benefit, the INSS ended up misplacing the aforementioned procedure, and the pensioner had to file two lawsuits so that, in the end, the local authority would attach photocopies of the misplaced documents. 2. Material damage cannot be surmised by the judge, but must be specified in the claim, under penalty of infringing the principle of restitutio in integro. 3) Moral damage can be claimed generically and arbitrated by the magistrate. It is not mere dissatisfaction, but a compensable inconvenience. 4) Appeal upheld in part, to reverse the lower court judgement and order the INSS to pay compensation for the moral damage experienced, setting the amount of compensation at R$ 20,000.00.[8]

If the applicant doesn't have a copy of a document that has been lost, its loss could be irreparable. If it was the administration that lost a certain document, it is clear that it is responsible, and the material and moral damage to those concerned is indisputable.

The loss of documents, even if only momentarily, may be subject to compensation for moral damage, and in some cases may constitute compensable moral damage.

When evidence disappears through no fault of the administration, as in the case of a catastrophe, the police report serves as proof and is the beginning of material evidence. The loss of a file is a harmful event that justifies moral damage.

2.2.9. Non-compliance with Decisions and Non-compliance with Precedents and Laws

Decisions that can no longer be reviewed or appealed, as well as court decisions that have already become final, must be complied with immediately. In accordance with article 64 of the CRPS Internal Regulations:

> The INSS is prohibited from refusing to comply with the final decisions of the Judgement Chambers, Appeals Boards and Judgement Panels of the Social Security Appeals Council (CRPS), reducing or extending their scope or executing them in a manner that contradicts or undermines their obvious meaning, under penalty of personal liability of the head of the sector in charge of executing the judgement. Sole Paragraph: The deadline for compliance with the provisions of the heading of this article is 30 (thirty) days from the date of receipt of the case at the source, at the end of which the interested party may represent the case to the immediately superior INSS authority, which will adopt the relevant measure (REGIMENTO INTERNO CRPS).

In this case, the sense of injustice is even greater, signalling moral damage, since failing to enforce an administrative or judicial decision, or delaying it, is not only a criminal offence but also liable to compensation for moral damage.

Article 103-A, paragraph 3 of the Federal Constitution states that: "An administrative act or judicial decision that contravenes the applicable precedent or that unduly applies it may be appealed to the Federal Supreme Court (STF), which, if well founded, shall annul the administrative act or set aside the judicial decision complained of, and shall order that another be issued with or without application of the precedent, as the case may be."

Failure to comply with these determinations implies expenses for the Public Administration and losses for the interested parties, with compensation being made for material damage, and it should be analysed whether the requirements for moral damage are present. In this sense:

> The INSS is prohibited from refusing to comply with the steps requested by the Social Security Appeals Board, as well as failing to comply with the final decisions of that board, reducing or extending their scope or executing them in a way that contradicts or jeopardises their obvious meaning (CASTRO, et.al, 2010, p.25).

The administration's claim of ignorance of the rule will not exempt it from liability, but failure to comply with clear precedents, regardless of the reason, represents non-compliance with its execution, for which reparation is due.

The INSS is linked to the Ministry of Social Security and has the obligation to grant and maintain social security benefits and services. It must respect the decisions of prosecutors and ministries in relation to the benefits of insured people, as well as respect rulings and laws and not use what is not provided for in them to delay or not make the payment of benefits due to insured people.

Thus, according to Castro, et.al (2010, p. 32) "the understanding on social security matters, contained in precedents of the Superior Courts, Regional Courts and Courts of Justice, as well as the Uniformisation Panels of the Special Federal Courts, play an important role in the understanding of the rules in force", and must be respected by the INSS.

CONCLUSION

This study was designed with the intention of studying and analysing the moral damage caused by social security benefits. As they are considered fundamental rights of a food nature, great care must be taken when denying them, since their denial gives rise to moral damage to the insured.

It is possible to observe the responsibility of the state, which is liable regardless of fault, but has the right to collect from the official who caused the damage.

The contributions made by insured people guarantee their subsistence when they need it, which is why the Social Security system must analyse each case before denying a benefit, since its function is to ensure the survival of the insured person.

The social security principles guarantee the insured the support they need to defend themselves in the event of an unjust refusal, whether from the local authority or another body that harms the insured.

Social security benefits and the defects that result from them show the failure of the state to supervise the social security authorities, which, due to these failures, which are not few, cause serious damage to the insured, who seek compensation for their loss through an action for compensation for moral damage.

Defects and undue denials that prevent the insured or their dependents from accessing social security benefits to which they would otherwise be entitled, constitute an offence against fundamental rights, causing psychological repercussions, as well as affecting their vital needs, resulting in the need to make reparation for moral damage.

Compensation for the damage will serve as a way of curbing the recurrence of abusive practices by the INSS, which should reflect better and better prepare its employees to serve the public, as well as prevent them from making mistaken decisions that affect the morale of the insured.

Therefore, this study has been carried out in the hope that it can contribute to alerting people to the need for greater transparency, efficiency and oversight by the state at all stages of the social security administrative process, in order to avoid unnecessary actions that harm insured people and their dependents.

REFERENCES

AGOSTINHO, Theodoro Vicente; SALVADOR, Sérgio Henrique. Moral damage in social security law. A necessary approach. Jus Navigandi, Teresina, year 18, n. 3652, 1 July 2013. Available at: <http://jus.com.br/artigos/24833>. Accessed on: 18 March 2014.

BALERA, Wagner. Social Security System. 4th Ed. São Paulo. LTR, 2006.

BANDEIRA DE MELO, Celso Antônio. Course in administrative law. 15. ed. rev. and updated. São Paulo: Malheiros, 2003.

BRAZIL. Judgement. Class: AC - CIVIL APPEAL. Case: 2007.72.04.001208-7 UF: SC. Date of Decision: 09/02/2010. Judging Body: Third Chamber. Full text. Source: D.E. 03/03/2010, Rapporteur Nicolau Konkel Júnior. Available at: < http://jurisprudencia.trf4.jus.br/pesquisa/resultado pesquisa.php> Accessed on 04 Mar. 2014.

. Judgement. Source: TRF-2. Class: AC - CIVIL APPEAL - 593774. Case: 200951018124368. UF: RJ. Judging Body: Second Specialised Panel. Decision date: 12/12/2013. Document: TRF-200286646. Source, E- DJF2R - Date: 17/01/2014. Rapporteur Federal Judge Messod Azulay Neto, Rapporteur for the Judgement, Federal Judge Marcelo Pereira da Silva, Voters, André Fontes, Marcelo Pereira da Silva. Available at: < http://jurisprudencia.trf2.jus.br/v1/search?q=Processo%3A+200951018124368+&clie nt=jurisprudencia&output=xmlno dtd&proxystylesheet=jurisprudencia&lr=lang en&e ntqrm=0&oe=UTF-8&ie=UTF- 8&ud=1 &exclude apps=1 &sort=date%3AD%3AS%3Ad1 &entqr=3&site=ementas&filt er=0&getfields=*&partialfields=&requiredfields=&asq=> Accessed 04 Mar. 2014.

. Judgement. Source: TRF-2. Class: AC - CIVIL APPEAL - 378260. Case: 200051070009397. UF: RJ. Judging Body: Seventh Specialised Panel. Decision date: 12/08/2009. Document: TRF-200217108. Rapporteur Federal Judge Salete Macclóz, Voters Sergio Feltrin Correa, Salete Macclóz, Theophilo Miguel, Reis Friede, Andrea Cunha Esmeraldo. Available at: < http://jurisprudencia.trf2.jus.br/v1/search?q=Processo%3A+200951018124368+&clie nt=jurisprudencia&output=xmlno dtd&proxystylesheet=jurisprudencia&lr=lang pt&e ntqrm=0&oe=UTF-8&ie=UTF-

8&ud=1 &exclude apps=1 &sort=date%3AD%3AS%3Ad1 &entgr=3&site=ementas&filt
er=0&getfields=*&partialfields=&requiredfields=&asq> Accessed 04 Mar. 2014.

. Judgement. Source: TRF-2. Class: APELREEX - APPEAL / NECESSARY REVIEW -
579464. Case: 201151018082435. UF: RJ. Judging Body: Second Specialised Panel.
Decision date: 26/06/2013. Document: TRF- 200278932. Rapporteur Federal Judge
Messod Azulay Neto, Voters Theophilo Miguel, André Fontes, Messod Azulay Neto,
Marcelo Pereira da Silva. Available at:
<http://jurisprudencia.trf2.jus.br/v1/search?q=Processo%3A+200951018124368+&cli
ent=jurisprudencia&output=xmlno dtd&proxystylesheet=jurisprudencia&lr=lang pt&
entgrm=0&oe=UTF-8&ie=UTF-
8&ud=1 &exclude apps=1 &sort=date%3AD%3AS%3Ad1 &entgr=3&site=ementas&filt
er=0&getfields=*&partialfields=&requiredfields=&asq> Accessed 04 Mar. 2014.

. Judgement. Source: TRF-2. Class: AC - CIVIL APPEAL - 349655. Case:
200151015352094. UF: RJ. Judging Body: Seventh Specialised Panel. Decision date:
17/06/2009. Document: TRF-200208394. Available at: <
http://jurisprudencia.trf2.jus.br/v1/search?q=Processo%3A+200951018124368+&clie
nt=jurisprudencia&output=xmlno dtd&proxystylesheet=jurisprudencia&lr=lang pt&e
ntgrm=0&oe=UTF-8&ie=UTF-
8&ud=1 &exclude apps=1 &sort=date%3AD%3AS%3Ad1 &entgr=3&site=ementas&filt
er=0&getfields=*&partialfields=&requiredfields=&asq> Accessed 04 Mar. 2014.

. CIVIL APPEAL. Date of Decision: 30/10/2002. Publication Date: 24/02/2003.
Rapporteur: André Fontes. Available at:
<http://jurisprudencia.trf2.jus.br/v1/search?q=Processo%3A+200951018124368+&cli
ent=jurisprudencia&output=xml_no_dtd&proxystylesheet=jurisprudencia&lr=lang_pt&
entgrm=0&oe=UTF-8&ie=UTF-
8&ud=1 &exclude_apps=1 &sort=date%3AD%3AS%3Ad1 &entgr=3&site=ementas&filt
er=0&getfields=*&partialfields=&requiredfields=&as_q> Accessed 04 Mar. 2014.

. Constitution (1988). Constitution of the Federative Republic of Brazil. Brasília, DF:
Federal Senate: Graphic Centre, 1988.

. DECREE-LAW NO. 5452, OF 1ST MAY 1943. Approves the Consolidation of Labour
Laws. National Congress, Brasília, 1st May 1943. Available at: <
http://www.planalto.gov.br/ccivil03/decreto-lei/del5452.htm > Accessed on 04 March
2014.

. LAW NO. 8.213, OF 24 JULY 1991. Provides for Social Security Benefit Plans and other measures. National Congress, Brasília, 24 July. 1991. Available at: < http://www.planalto.gov.br/ccivil_03/leis/l8213cons.htm > Accessed on 04 March 2014.

. LAW No. 10.406, OF 10 JANUARY 2002. Establishes the Civil Code. National Congress, Brasília, 10 January 2002. Available at: <http://www.planalto.gov.br/ccivil_03/leis/2002/l10406.htm> Accessed on 04 March 2014.

. LAW N° 11.430 - OF 26 DECEMBER 2006. Amends Laws 8.213, of 24 July 1991, and 9.796, of 5 May 1999, increases the value of social security benefits; and repeals Provisional Measure 316, of 11 August 2006; provisions of Laws 8.213, of 24 July 1991, 8.444, of 20 July 1992, and Provisional Measure 2.187-13, of 24 August 2001; and Law 10.699, of 9 July 2003. National Congress. 26 December 2006. Available at : < http://www3.dataprev.gov.br/sislex/paginas/42/2006/11430.htm> Accessed 04 Mar. 2014.

. Ordinance 548 of 13 September 2011. Approves the Internal Regulations of the Social Security Appeals Council - CRPS. Ministry of Social Security Office of the Minister. Available at: < http://www.previdencia.gov.br/arquivos/office/1_121220-102751-326.pdf> Accessed on 04 March 2014.

. REsp 1026088 / SC. SPECIAL APPEAL. 2008/0023141-0. Reporting Justice Francisco Falcão (1116). Judgement Body T1 - First Panel. Date of Judgement 03/04/2008. Publication Date/Source, DJe, 23/04/2008. Available at: http://www.jusbrasil.com.br/diarios/63100665/djpe-17-12-2013-pg-942 Accessed on: 04 Mar. 2014.

BITTAR, Carlos Alberto. Civil Reparation for Moral Damage. 3ª Ed. São Paulo: RT, 1997.

CAHALI, Yussef Said. Moral Damage. 2nd Ed. São Paulo. Editora Revista dos Tribunais, 1999.

CAMPOS, Wânia Alice Ferreira Lima. Moral damage in social security law: Doctrine, legislation, case law and practice. Curitiba: Juruá, 2011.

CAVALIERI FILHO, Sérgio. Civil Liability Programme. Ed. Atlas. São Paulo, 2009.

DI PIETRO, Maria Sylvia Zanella. Administrative Law. 22. ed. São Paulo: Atlas, 2009.

DUARTE, Marina Vasques. Social Security Law. 7th Ed. Porto Alegre, Verbo Jurídico,

2011.

ESTEVES, Paulo, others. Moral Damage. São Paulo. Editora Fisco e Contribuinte Ltda., 1999.

FARINELI, Alexsandro Menezes, MASCHIETO, Fábia. Social Security Moral Damage Theory and Practice. São Paulo. Mundo Jurídico, 2011.

HENK, Maria Helena Pinheiro. Dignity of the Human Person and Moral Damage in the Scope of the Right to Social Security Benefits. Electronic proceedings of the III International Law Symposium: material and effective dimensions of fundamental rights. Available at: <http://editora.unoesc.edu.br/index.php/simposiointernacionaldedireito> Accessed on 20 March 2014.

LAZZARI, João Batista, CASTRO, Carlos Alberto Pereira. Social Security Law. Florianópolis. Conceito Editorial, 2010.

MARTINEZ, Wladimir Novaes. Moral Damage in Social Security Law. São Paulo, LTR, 2005.

ZIMMERMANN, Diego. Moral Damage in Social Security Law. Available at http://bibliodigital.unijui.edu.br:8080/xmlui/bitstream/handle/123456789/1105/Diego%20Zimmermann.pdf?sequence=1 >Accessed on 20 Mar. 2014.

I want morebooks!

Buy your books fast and straightforward online - at one of world's fastest growing online book stores! Environmentally sound due to Print-on-Demand technologies.

Buy your books online at
www.morebooks.shop

Kaufen Sie Ihre Bücher schnell und unkompliziert online – auf einer der am schnellsten wachsenden Buchhandelsplattformen weltweit! Dank Print-On-Demand umwelt- und ressourcenschonend produziert.

Bücher schneller online kaufen
www.morebooks.shop

Printed by Books on Demand GmbH, Norderstedt / Germany